Bedtime for Toddlers!

Here's to no more bedtime woes!
Good Luck ....;
Lois Heirl

Bedtime for Toddlers!

Lois Kleint, M.A., Ed.
Early Childhood Specialist

Creating Gifted Kids Enterprises
San Diego, California

www.creatinggiftedkids.com

Published by
Creating Gifted Kids Enterprises
San Diego, CA
© 2005 Lois Kleint

ISBN 0-9716399-1-4

Jean Kleint, *Editor*

Ann Huisman
Cover, Book Design, Prepress
ahadesigner@cox.net

Printed in China

*This book is dedicated to
all the little toddlers who attended my schools.*

You taught me much over the years.

Contents at a Glance

Introduction

Many young parents experience difficulties with their toddlers at bedtime, and most don't know what to do about it or where to turn. This book was created to help you find solutions. In it, you will learn answers for such situations as:

- *Getting your toddler to bed peacefully with a bedtime routine*
- *Overcoming nighttime fears*
- *Taming temper tantrums*
- *Making the transition from crib to bed*
- *Staying dry all night*
- *Training your toddler to cooperate in additional childhood behaviors*

Creating a child's behavior patterns begins at birth. When you first hold your tiny, newborn infant, you are so in love with this adorable little creation. As the days unfold with your little treasure, you are willing to give up almost every area of your personal life to be a good parent.

Then, as time goes by and your tiny baby grows into a toddler, you can begin to feel as if you don't even have a life. Around the age of two, he begins to assert his own little independent self in negative ways. You may find yourself giving in to your child's demands and allowing the child to direct you, instead of the other way around. With this encroaching negative behavior, he begins to "rule the roost." This change can sneak up on you, and before you know what has happened, you really *don't* have a life of your own.

However, when you recognize your own feelings of frustration and helplessness, you have reached an all-important first step: seeing the need to help *yourself* so that you can help your child. You may recognize your child's behavior as unpleasant, and that you *need* it to change. But without the knowledge of *how* to train and guide your toddler, you may feel trapped.

Here's the solution.

With this book as your guide, you **can** train your toddler to cooperate with you and develop a positive bedtime routine–within just a few short days.

These time-tested techniques, involving principles of positive behavioral training, were developed from practical experience with hundreds of toddlers throughout a 15-year period in my own private nursery school. Time and time again, we witnessed parents' excitement as their toddlers' behavior changed from negative to positive. We have seen these wonderful results occur 99% of the time when these principles and methods were applied.

This teaching is based on established research concerning development from birth through three years of age. This phase in your child's life provides opportunities crucial to specific types of learning. These early years are optimal for learning new ideas and skills, and establishing positive behavior patterns within the child.

The positive approach to child-rearing described in this book involves the principle of teaching your child compliance to simple commands, *without* the old-fashioned methods of force or intimidation.

The act of teaching your toddler simple commands and walking him through a few days of "training time" to master bedtime problems can have far-reaching effects. Requiring cooperation in this area of his or her life will not only begin to give *you* a life (once household peace has been established at bedtime); this training will also serve as a foundation for your child's success in other areas.

Wise parents know the importance of instilling specific values in children at a very early age, and that doing so will go a long way toward preventing problems later in life. As we pay attention to this crucial time in early childhood for setting positive behavior patterns, our children can bypass many of the problems that plague adults in our society today. Setting requirements while your child is two years old will result in a well-adjusted, delightful little person, one who can grow up into an equally well-adjusted, functional adult. This book will show you how.

In order to apply the techniques for any and all of these behavior changes, parents need to understand the *principles* of behavior specific to this time in your child's life. With this understanding, you will know how to consistently apply these methods for any situation that arises with your toddler. The principles taught in this book apply wonderfully to a small child's transition from crib to bed, as well as helping a child to willingly stay in bed at night, to stay dry without bed wetting, etc. The result is that any toddler can have an easy transition for learning to get to sleep peacefully and overcome troublesome bedtime behaviors. In addition to the overall principles, there are specific techniques for each bedtime behavior in the chapters that follow.

It is my hope that the lives of parents and children everywhere will be greatly enriched by this book. Not only can the negative behavior of the "terrible two's" be reversed; it can also be prevented. When children are exposed from birth to these positive behavior patterns, they never learn the negative behavior in the first place, and never have to unlearn negative traits as adults.

May your toddler become a greater joy, and may bedtime become a pleasure at your house, as you learn to train your little one in these simple techniques. May you join the many other parents who have learned that bedtime can be fun for everyone.

Lois Kleint, M.A., Ed. – Early Childhood Specialist – San Diego, CA 2005

Preparing Yourself First

In order for your child to have success with new bedtime behaviors, you as a parent need to first prepare *yourself*. This includes learning a new mindset and techniques for training and directing your child into positive behavior patterns. This knowledge will give you a sense of confidence and empower you to work with your child.

We recommend that you read through this entire book before beginning to work with your toddler.

As you read this first chapter, you will prepare yourself with a positive mental attitude and learn how to plan a "training time" for many behaviors. Here are some key principles to adopt as a mindset for success.

1. *Know What You Want.*	It is important to first consider *your* needs as the parent, recognize how *you* feel about your child's bedtime behavior, and know what *you* want from him at bedtime. This *first* step is about you, and your needs as a parent – it is not about your child's behavior or his lack of willingness.

Know that your child's behavior *will* begin to change, as *you* learn this new way of thinking with the step-by-step procedures in this book.

It is important that *you* feel confident, knowing yourself and respecting your own needs. You need to be firm in your own mind, recognizing that:

- You *should* expect your toddler to cooperate when it is bedtime.

- You *do not* have to allow his negative behavior.

- There *are specific things* that you can do to help your child into positive behavior and make bedtime pleasant for all.

It is a general tendency of parents to believe that a toddler *cannot* be expected to cooperate at an early age. However, the truth is that your toddler knows exactly what he is doing when he misbehaves; parents are misguided when believing that a young child does not understand what he is being asked to do.

This tender age is the best window of opportunity for teaching cooperation and compliance to simple commands.

However, if you are not firm within *yourself* about what you want and expect from your toddler, then you will not give clear direction, and he will not know what to expect or how to behave. This does not mean you need to be harsh with the child, but rather that you need to make a decision and stick with that decision.

2.
Give Your Child the Security of Direction.

The undirected child will automatically tend toward negative behavior. Parents need to tell their child what they expect by giving simple commands. In order for your child to learn a new behavior, he needs your guidance, nurturing and encouragement. Early childhood is a time of social referencing, and your toddler is counting on *you* to tell him what is right and how to be in any given situation. At this stage, your job is to make decisions *for* him, and not leave decisions to the child. Giving toddlers choices and options on how to behave only causes confusion and insecurity.

While some experts advocate that it is best to allow the child to "take the lead," work with hundreds of toddlers and parents has shown the opposite to be true.

Small children of this age need specific direction. That is what this book is all about. **Your toddler needs the security of direction from you.** Your positive encouragement and guidance will shape his behavior. The security derived from being directed at an early age gives the child the foundation for learning to make his own decisions later on. You will begin to give him more and more choices as he grows older. For right now, the security for a small child comes from having the parent *tell* him what to do and how to think about things.

Thus, this book does not advocate a child-centered home with the child's needs ruling the whole household and creating chaos and frustration. Rather, these methods can create a family-centered home, where everyone's needs are considered and each member of the family is flowing together, including the toddler. By giving him direction, your toddler can be trained to cooperate in harmony with the entire family's needs.

As an example of this principle of parental guidance by giving simple commands, at bedtime you will say to your two-year-old: "It is time to get ready for bed. Come to the bathroom and stand on your stool so we can brush your teeth." You first tell your child what is to happen, and then state a simple one-sentence command, clearly and convincingly. **Never give a command unless you plan to carry through.** In this example, you will then take the child's little hand, lead him to the bathroom, and stand with him as he steps up on the stool. Do not give the child the option of going elsewhere or doing anything else at that moment. You can do this by carefully guiding his physical actions to do what you have requested.

In other words, **as soon as you give a command, you need to physically walk your toddler through the action** – in this case, by taking his little hand or actually picking him up and taking him to do the instruction you have given him.

Likewise, it is the *parent* who should determine when the child is developmentally ready for each new behavioral change. Watch for clues that it is time for a transition, but don't put it off by leaving it up to the child to learn a new behavior on his own. For example, your child does not know when it is time for him to make the transition from crib to bed; the parent must make this decision for the child. At about age two is a good time for this particular transition. A second birthday is often a good time for a child to receive his new bed.

These principles are discussed further in later chapters.

3.
Make a Commitment. In order to create positive behavior patterns in your child, the key elements are your mindset, commitment, and resolve; you must make a **decision** and a determination to train your child, realizing that you will need to commit concentrated time and effort with your toddler. Requiring his cooperation takes a vigilance and consistency. However, this training time does not go on forever. You will be pleased to find surprising results within a few short days.

4.
Maintain an Attitude of Confidence and Enthusiasm. Toddlers are sensitive to the subtle messages that parents transmit, whether positive or negative, spoken or unspoken. Whatever is in the parent's attitude comes through; the child takes his cues from you.

Therefore, it is important that you feel confident about what *your own* needs are, before attempting to training your toddler. By mastering the simple strategies in this book, you will be enabled to project confidence and faith to your child. Realize that **it is up to you**, the parent, if the toddler is to have success in his new behavior. **It is not up to the child.**

You will need to create an environment and atmosphere of success for him. He will need your support and guidance throughout an initial training period for creating each new behavior pattern. He will also need your continued guidance for a short time after the initial "training time" in order to maintain the new behavior until it is a set pattern. He cannot do it on his own. By using the powerful tools of encouragement, praise and reward, you will be able to help the child into a sense of success and self-esteem. As you learn these skills, your child will sense your excitement, key off of your enthusiasm, and trust your belief in him. This sense of trust will become a part of him, as will the desired behavior.

5.
Plan Ahead for a Three-day Training Period.

To do this, you will need to give bedtime training your focus for at least three consecutive evenings, nighttimes, and naptimes.

Because it is imperative that you give this training your full attention, it is important to choose a time when you are well, rested and feeling on top, and a time when your child is also feeling well and not stressed.

Your first step is to decide on the day to start this three-day training period. Some parents choose a three-day weekend.

During those three days, plan to:

- Have your mate or someone else take care of other children in the home at bedtime.

- Spend extra time with the child you are training, both during the day and in the evening. This should be unhurried, leisure time and fun time.

Once you have prepared *yourself* by adopting this mindset, we can go on to the next chapters on how to prepare your toddler. We'll discuss how to establish a bedtime routine, training for a new behavior, and how to help your child make the transition from crib to bed, as an example of how to prepare him for the other types of bedtime behaviors discussed later on.

Establishing a Bedtime Routine 2

*L*ittle children love and need routine. Knowing what will happen next gives the child a sense of security. Before adjusting a nighttime behavior, such as switching your child from his crib to a new "big boy" or "big girl" bed, it will be important to have already established your own unique bedtime routine for the child. This brief 15-minute to 30-minute preparation time may include some or all of the following steps:

- **Brushing his teeth**

- **Going to the potty**

- **Bathing**

- **Putting on pajamas and putting away his clothing**

- **Getting a drink of water**

- **Singing a good-night song**

- **Reading a special bedtime story while on Mommy's or Daddy's lap**

- **Saying his prayers**

- **Snuggle time**

- **A good-night kiss and hug**

- **Tucking in and saying goodnight**

Whichever steps you choose to do from this list, do these *same steps in the same order* each night from now on, and establish this routine for at least several days to ensure that your child knows what comes next. After about three days of this very consistent routine, parents find that much of the resistance to bedtime is already eliminated. Then, a new change, such as the transition from crib to bed, becomes an easy step.

To establish a routine, you will need to physically walk your child through each activity for bedtime, and give very simple commands with follow-through and simple conversation about what comes next.

Here is an example of how to implement such a routine:

1. *Decide on Bedtime.*	Make the decision about what time you want the child to go to bed, and *keep the same bedtime every night.*
2. *Give Warning*	Begin by giving your toddler ample warning time to let him know when it will soon be bedtime. When it's near the time, say to the child:

"In five minutes, it will be time to pick up your toys and start getting ready for bedtime." (A two-year-old will understand this concept.)

3. *Use a Timer.*	Try using a timer to signify that his playtime is finished: • After your verbal warning, have the child help you set a timer for five more minutes of playtime. When the

timer goes off, immediately begin to wrap up his evening activities.

- Work with him to put toys away, etc. Don't expect him to be able to do this on his own. Make it fun.

- Even very young children like timers instead of Mom's nagging; it is easier on the child as well as the parent. Be sure the timer goes off the same time each evening, and that cleanup and bedtime routine follow immediately after the timer.

Your conversation during this time should be pleasant and unhurried:

"Oh! There's the timer! It's time to put away the toys and get ready for bed! I'll help you put away your toys. We had a wonderful day today. I am getting so sleepy. You are getting sleepy. All the toys are getting sleepy. They can go to sleep right here on the toy shelf. Let's put them away for the night," etc.

4.
Offer a
Bedtime
Snack

Once the toys have been picked up and put away for the evening, offer a small bedtime snack, such as fruit or cheese. Have the child eat his snack in the same place at the same time every night, so that it becomes a routine that he looks forward to. Keep liquids to a minimum before bedtime, however, and avoid sugary treats.

Conversation for snack time might be:

"Good! All the toys are put away. Now it is time for your bedtime snack. Let's go to the kitchen. Sit down here in your chair at the table, and I will get your little snack."

Be aware that your conversation is guiding your child from one activity to another. Also, during the toddler phase, you will need to continually, physically accompany the child to the next activity. *Don't expect him to do this on his own at this age.* At snack time, choose the child's food for him, and simply set the snack in front of him. If he does not care to eat, don't make a big deal of it; simply guide him into the next part of his bedtime routine.

5.
Brush Teeth, Bathe, and Use Toilet.

Accompany your child to the bathroom and help him brush teeth, bathe, and use the toilet. Talk your child through these activities, making this a positive, pleasant time. Tell him he is getting sleepy, and it will soon be time to go to his room to put on pajamas and go to sleep.

6.
Put on Pajamas.

Take the child to his room and help him put on pajamas.

7.
Put Teddy or Dolly to Sleep.

Your child can learn to go to sleep through the practice of teaching his own teddy bear or doll to sleep in its own bed. What your child teaches, he will learn and internalize.

Have a doll bed or simple sleeping spot set up somewhere in the room ahead of time. At bedtime, teach your child to tuck in his companion, stroke and talk to it until it "falls asleep," and then leave it in its own bed. In fact, you may want to have your child practice the entire bedtime procedure with the bear or doll in order for your toddler to learn what you are requiring of him at bedtime.

8.
Tuck Your Toddler in Bed.

Then help the child to get into his own bed. Tuck him in the covers and talk to him. This is the perfect time to tell him how *special and important* he is. This will go a long way later in his life.

9.
Snuggle With Your Toddler.

Snuggle next to your child and read a story, tell a story, or simply talk about the day. Stroke him as you talk in a quiet, soothing voice to settle him down, telling him how sleepy he is and that he will not even want to get up until morning. This winding down of the evening's routine should include hugs and kisses.

10.
Stay Next to the Child Until He Falls Asleep.

To establish this settling down time resulting in actual sleep for your toddler, it requires that you *remain present with the child.* You have to **be there** until he falls soundly asleep. At this point, pull up a chair and sit next to your toddler. Remain present with the child, seated very close, where he can see you and you can lay your hands gently on him, until you are sure that he is soundly asleep.

This may not be required for too many days until he will go to sleep easily by virtue of the same routine and expected pattern. For most children, your presence will be required for only a few days until they establish the pattern of trust.

Do this same routine in the same order every night, and preferably at the same time. Making it something he can *always* depend on will give the child a feeling of being secure and safe.

⟶➤●◄⟵

Training for a New Behavior 3

For your child to learn a new behavior and to experience success with it, he needs to first know how to think about it. How will he know unless he is taught? *You* can teach him how to think, and how to act by your consistent nurturing encouragement, and that includes how to go to sleep peacefully at night.

We suggest that you take a few days to a week to prepare your child before initiating an actual three-day training time for behavioral transitions. Here are the key elements of preparation that we have found to be imperative in dealing with bedtime for the very young child.

1.

Initiate a New Behavior Pattern by Talking About It Beforehand.

Once you get a consistent routine for nighttime, you can begin preparation for a three-day training time for a new behavior, such as transitioning to a new bed. This preparation will involve a few days of pep talk before the transition.

Talk to your child and involve him in everything you are thinking concerning the upcoming changes. This "pep talk" allows him to know ahead of time what he can expect, and it will create enthusiasm in the child. Keep it simple.

When you talk to him, be creative in discussing the new behavior. Talk to him and motivate him toward what you want him to do. Express your faith in him. For example, tell your child:

"In a few days, it will be time for you to get a new "big boy (or big girl) bed."

"You are so wonderful, you are getting so big now. It will be so fun to sleep in your new bed!"

The goal is to have this new behavior in his thinking before you start an actual training period or transition, and to help him know how he needs to think about the new situation.

This is an important principle: Small children need to know ahead of time what will happen, and to be talked through events before they take place. No surprises!

2.
Involve the Child in Preparing for New Surroundings.

During the same few days that you begin talking to him about his new behavior, plan to involve the child in preparations for his new bed, setting up his bedroom, getting new pajamas, etc.

Arranging for a new bed - If you purchase the bed, take the child to the store with you to buy it. It is best if the child is available to watch and help when the bed is delivered and set up. If it is received from another family or another room in your house, involve the child in moving the bed into his room.

Pajamas and bed sheets - This is a good time to go shopping with the child for new pajamas, new bed sheets, etc. It is another opportunity to emphasize the privilege and specialness of getting big enough to have a new bed of his very own. Make a "big deal" out of this preparation; find a favorite cartoon or animal motif for his room, including sheets, pajamas, etc. This will give him incentive for cooperating. Express your excitement for fixing up his room so that he will be proud of his new surroundings.

<u>Old crib</u> - Be sure you do not take apart the crib until the day the new bed arrives.

<u>Create excitement</u> - Throughout the days of preparation time, talk with your toddler about his coming "Big Day" when you (and he) will remove his crib, bring in the new bed, fix up his room, and allow him to wear his new pajamas.

3.
Draw Pictures or Take Photos. You cannot be too detailed in your description of how your child is going to be in this new situation. With the child watching, draw a picture of a child lying in his new bed, and have him color it while you talk to him. When he is finished coloring, help him hang the picture over the location for his new bed. You might also take a photo of your child sleeping, and hang it on the wall or hang up magazine pictures of a sleeping child. This type of visualization is especially necessary for the young child or the "difficult" child, as it will help him better understand what is expected of him in the new situation.

———⟶⟩●⟨⟵———

Now that you know how to prepare yourself and prepare your child, let's go on to procedures for the actual three-day training period.

Transitioning from Crib to Bed 4

Following are the specific procedures for the three-day training period that you have set aside to help your child transition from crib to bed. As previously mentioned, many of the procedures can also be applied to other bedtime behaviors, several of which are discussed in the chapters that follow.

Note that naptime during this training should follow similar procedures. Of course, naptime will involve a simpler routine.

1.
Talk All During the Day.
On the day you begin this training, continue to talk to your child all day long about what he will be doing at bedtime that evening. Tell him over and over what you expect of him. State your words as a fact in the present tense, with enthusiasm, kindness and trust in the child's ability. For example, here's a pep talk when you are transitioning from the crib to the bed:

- *"You LOVE your new bed!"*

- *"You are a big boy (or a big girl) now."*

- *"You are so lucky, you are going to sleep in a new big boy (or big girl) bed!"*

- *"We are going to take your crib apart today, and put it away, so that we have a place for your new bed in your room."*

- *"Where your crib is now, we are going to put a new big boy bed, just for you, because you are getting so big."*

- *"You are growing up; you are too big for a crib now. You will love your new bed!"*

- *"You are going to sleep in your new bed tonight, and you are going to stay in your new bed all night, you love it so much."*

- *"You are not even going to get up off your bed, not even one time, you are going to be so sleepy, and you have such a special bed to sleep in, you love to go to sleep."*

- *"You are so special, and I know that you won't even want to get off your bed when it is time go to sleep."*

- *"You are going to be so sleepy and tired that you will go to sleep right away. You won't even fuss."*

- *"See these little feet? They are so wonderful. They won't even think of getting out of the covers and putting themselves on the floor after you have gone to bed. They will love to snuggle under the covers in your new bed, and stay there all night."*

This much conversation throughout the day may seem like overkill, but not for a toddler. How will your child know how to think unless you teach him?

Be creative. Think of things to say that will fit your own child's situation to encourage him. Keep it positive, and keep it in the present tense, with conversation so suggestive of how things are going to be and how he is going to think, that he will automatically believe you and carry through with the behavior you are describing.

2.
Put Your Child in Bed.

On the first night, do the usual routine to help the child get ready for bed, sticking with the normal bedtime procedures that you have already established. Meanwhile, tell your child how he is going to be in his new behavior as he prepares for bed:

- *"Remember when Mommy (or Daddy) talked to you all day long today, and said you would not even put one foot on the floor after I tucked you in tonight?"*

- *"You are going to stay in bed and go right to sleep, just like Mommy said."*

- *"You will want to close your little eyes, and you won't even move or wiggle you will be SO sleepy."*

- *"You love your new bed."*

- *"See the picture you colored? This child is staying in his bed, just like you."*

Once the bedtime routine is completed, tuck the child into his new bed.

After he is in bed, *do not allow* the child to talk you into one more drink, one more potty time, etc. Make sure that these needs have been met beforehand within your routine so that he does not need to get out of bed. This allows you to be confident in your insistence, so that you can be firm but kind and gentle in saying, *"No, it's time to go to sleep now."* **It is important at this point not to waiver but to stick with the plan.**

3.
Avoid Stimulation. Once the routine is completed and it is time to settle down to actually sleep, there should not be any kind of further stimulation in the room. The child will be distracted from sleep if he continues to hear music playing or if he has any toys or teddy bears in his bed. Remember, Bear has been put in his own bed. Help your child relate to it as a "sleepy" bear who is going to sleep too, and who is too sleepy to play. Your toddler will be more settled if he is not distracted with toys or hearing noises.

If you have carefully taken care of all of the bedtime procedures leading up to the actual time to go to sleep, making sure that the child is actually sleepy and relaxed, there will be no excuse for getting up for any reason once the child has been tucked in.

This sets a pattern. Repeat it *three* consecutive nights and naptimes, and it will become an internalized behavior for the child. The child realizes, "Mommy really *expects* me to go to sleep now. I know what to do next; I will go to sleep." Completing the same routine each night leads to sleepiness at about the same time each night and creates the associated thought that "it is time for me to go to sleep."

This may surprise parents, *but you can actually induce your child to go to sleep by how you speak to him, and by repeating his routine.*

4.
Stay in His Room Until He Falls Soundly Asleep.

To reiterate what has been previously discussed: During the training time, it is important to stay in his room until he goes to sleep. In this way, he knows that you mean what you say, and that you are not going to **let** him get out of his bed even one time, no matter what. **Help the child have the success of not getting out of his bed.** You are on his side, and you want him to have success. You must be there, on duty, and not allow him to get up for any reason. Do not let him get out of bed even the first time, and do not sympathize with his requests for additional visits to the potty, drink of water, kisses for Daddy, etc.

Pull up a chair next to his bed and sit close to him. Do *not* lie down with your child in his bed at this "falling asleep" point; leave snuggle time as a part of the earlier routine. As he falls asleep, however, you will sit next to his new bed. This will also ensure that he is not awakened when you get up to leave his room.

Tell him that you will sit beside him until he is asleep, and then you will go to sleep in your own bed later on. The message you want to convey at this point is that the child does not need to have Mommy on his bed; he is a big boy now and can sleep alone in his new bed. Mommy will be there till he sleeps, and available if he calls for her during the night.

Gently put your hand on his little head or on his shoulder. This helps him to pull inside himself so that he is not tempted to move around. It prevents him from even lifting his head off his pillow.

Be assured that if a small child is prepared for bedtime in this way and is required to lie quietly, he can settle into sleepiness very quickly. This process is teaching the child how to put *himself* to sleep.

5.
Reward Your Child. On this first night when you tuck him into his new bed, you will tell your child that there will be a little present on his bed when he wakes in the morning. Tell him if he does not put his little feet on the floor to get out of bed all night, not even one time, then he will see a present on his bed when he wakes up.

Make sure beforehand that the little reward is placed in his room somewhere out of sight. Then, after he is soundly asleep, place it at the foot of his bed so that he can see it when he first wakes up. This is a big thing in the child's mind. Wrap the little gift to make it special and fun. Be creative! Play it up! Remember: *Reward is a powerful tool.*

Give a reward only the first one or two nights. By the third night, take the attitude that staying in his new bed is now expected. It is not an option. In this way, he will not become dependent upon a reward in order to go to sleep. Instead, he will have established a pattern, not knowing there is any other way to behave.

6.
Require Compliance. | Parents can tend to leave it up to the child to decide whether or not he will comply with what he has been asked to do. Avoid this mistake. **It is not up to the child to decide.** You must require his compliance, by your actions, your words, your attitude, *and* your thoughts of trust and confidence in him.

Frequently, parents instruct their child to stay in bed, and then leave the room before the child is asleep. Then when the little child gets out his bed to go find out what Mommy and Daddy are doing, the parent thinks he should punish the child's "disobedience." This is a mistake on the parent's part, because punishment does nothing to train the child into positive behavior.

The idea instead is that you don't allow negative behavior to begin with; you do not let him make the mistake of "disobedience" in the first place. This means that you are there with him, guiding him and requiring his compliance *until* he falls asleep.

7.
Block Negative Behavior.

If you block the negative behavior before it happens, punishment will never be necessary. Be assured that it will usually take only two or three evenings of this type of consistent monitoring in order to establish a positive pattern for a new behavior. **Little children learn very quickly by routine and repetition.**

Remember, if your child is to have success in this new behavior (staying in bed), you need to stick to an effective plan. This means:

- **You are THERE; you do not leave his bedside until he is soundly asleep.**

- **You do not let the negative behavior (getting up) happen even one time.** Otherwise, you will have to begin all over again.

8.
Praise Your Child.

Continue to give loads of verbal reinforcement and praise throughout the following days until the pattern is set. Tell him many times throughout the day:

- *"You are so special."*
- *"You didn't even get out of your bed one time!"*
- *"You were so sleepy."*
- *"You stayed in your bed and went right to sleep."*

9.
Avoid Being Negative; Keep it Positive.

This is an important principle. Realize that most children are not able, at age two, to compute in their little minds, "What *do* I do?" Your toddler may know what *not* to do because you often say "No." But unless he is told what *to do* instead, there will be a void where there should be positive, creative direction.

This is why you say, *"You are going to stay in your bed once I have put you in your bed. You are going to go sound asleep."* If you need to say "no" to a toddler, then in the same breath, tell your child what he *should* do: *"No, you are not going to get out of your bed. You are going to stay right here. It is sleep time now, you are sleepy, and you will not even get up."* It is very important to keep your conversation and attitude positive. Little children believe and respond very well to this type of suggestive talk.

10.
Be Consistent.

Being *consistent* is the only way you can help your child develop the positive pattern of staying in his bed once you have put him there. If he is never allowed to get out of his new bed, he will not know any other behavior for that situation. This requires consistent parental vigilance for a few days.

On the other hand, **inconsistency encourages misbehavior!** If the child is sometimes allowed to get out of bed, and other times not, your inconsistency develops the wrong behavior pattern, and your training is of no avail.

Picture yourself as a toddler, receiving mixed signals that allow different behavior at different times; this breeds a sense of confusion and insecurity. **The child needs the security of *your* direction**, knowing exactly how much he can or cannot do. **By setting limits, and carrying through, you develop a positive relationship of respect with your child.** With this type of prevention method and careful consistency, there will be no need for parents to spank, hit, yell, threaten, or become dictatorial and reactive out of frustration.

Consistency is the *major* key in setting positive behavior patterns. The new behavior becomes a pattern very quickly for a small child, particularly when the child realizes in his little mind that this is not optional. The child needs to know that neither Mommy nor Daddy are push-overs. They sense that you mean what you say, and you will remain consistent. This does not require you to be unkind or harsh, only consistent and firm within your own mind about what you want to require.

These procedures, principles and attitudes will help you in setting any new behavior pattern for your young child.

This might seem like a lot of work for parents, but remember it is only necessary for a few short days; this is a very small price to pay for creating peaceful bedtimes for years to come!

<hr>

Overcoming Nighttime Fears 5

$\mathcal{E}$arly childhood fears of all types develop in young children for no apparent reason; little children simply perceive the world through their lack of experience, and they can become fearful of almost anything.

One particular fear for a toddler is that of staying in his own room at night. It is important for parents to know that this fear (and almost any other childhood fear) can be quickly and easily unlearned by the guidance of a wise parent, especially when a child is very young. You can also help prevent bedtime fears from developing to begin with.

A basic principle used by psychologists in dealing with fears is the concept of, "do the fear." In other words, with assistance, a person can often be walked through the process of doing the thing he fears, and discover that there is nothing to fear.

There is a way to tenderly walk your child out of his fear and to **ease** him into the desired behavior, making him feel secure, loved, and comforted. With consistency and your support, being there for him, your child will easily learn that there is no need to be afraid.

Generally speaking, however, when a young child has existing fears, the parent tends to be sympathetic. Mom or Dad will give in to the child's withdrawal and become resigned to putting up with a toddler's balking, fearfulness, and resulting negative behavior. Allowing this behavior is not the way to help a child overcome his fear; in fact, it strengthens his fear. Don't consign your child to live in his fear, steeped in it until it becomes an automatic response and a way of life for him later on.

What can parents do instead?

By using the example of teaching your toddler to stay in bed at night, let's take a look at dealing with childhood fears.

1. *Create a Comfortable and Safe Atmosphere.*	First, deal with the physical environment that might be making your toddler fearful. In the case of nighttime fears, the goal is to make your toddler love his bedroom; make him feel like his room is a wonderful place – a safe, peaceful, comfortable place, a fun place where he loves to be.

Talk with your toddler and determine if there is anything in the room that looks scary at night. Then make any physical changes in the room to help with this. For example, it is best for a young child to avoid sleeping under a window; also, he needs to be able to see the door from his bed. It may also be important for him to have a night light or a hallway light left on. Also of importance is the presence of favorite toys or stuffed animals, and the absence of scary toys, animals, pictures, or other disturbing visual images in his room. Study his room in the dark; talk with him about his room, and make the necessary physical changes to remove anything that to him might become a scary image at night.

2.

Talk Him Through It.

Remember that a young child will believe anything his parents tell him. All during the day, be positive in your speech; be enthusiastic about him being able to sleep peacefully at night. Talk to him several times a day. Tell him you will leave the night light on when he goes to bed. Tell him you will leave his door open so that you can hear him if he calls; tell him you will come anytime he calls for you at night (and do so). Ask him not to get out of his bed, but to simply call for you. Hug him during these daytime talks, and help him to be calm about bedtime. Give him the assurance that Mommy and Daddy would never let anything happen to him because "we love you so much!" Bedtime should be a wonderful time for him, and your attitude is what will create a feeling of security.

3.

Follow Bedtime Procedures Already Discussed.

Be sure that your child has a nighttime routine, and tell him how to think about bedtime. Make bedtime fun for him, as discussed. Following the procedures in the previous chapters will go a long way toward alleviating nighttime fears.

4.

Put Your Child to Bed at Night and Sit by His Bed Until He Falls Asleep.

Don't expect a fearful child to fall asleep by himself. Again, follow the procedures already mentioned.

5.
Respond to Your Child Immediately in the Middle of Night.

If your child cries out in fear, you will need to get up and immediately go to his room. If he gets out of bed to look for Mommy or Daddy, pick him up and carry him immediately back to his room; he will be disoriented and still half asleep, so do not get into any conversation with him (about why he needs to stay in his bed, etc.). Simply take your child back to his bedroom; turn on a light if needed, hug him tightly, and speak calmly to comfort him. It is this quick response, and getting the child back to his bed, that will say more than anything you verbalize. Stay in his room, sitting beside him as you stroke his head, place your hand on his shoulder, etc.

It is important for him to return to his **own** bed, to overcome the fear. At this point, do not give in to your own frustration or lack of sleep; stick with it, and get the child back to sleep in his own bed. If you tuck him in with you in your bed at this time, you will reinforce the fear, and undo everything you have been creating toward the goal of staying in his own bed.

It is a different matter altogether to put him in your bed for snuggle time in the early evening (at your initiative, and your timing). However, to get him to sleep at night, and for the middle-of-the-night wake-ups, it is important to get him back to his own room.

6.

Deal With Nightmares Carefully.

If a child wakes because of scary dreams, take special care to get the child back to sleep. Pick him up and hold him, turn on a light, walk around the house, and, in the case of awakening with nightmares, you can distract him with conversation or activity until he shakes off the dream and settles down. Again, he will be disoriented and still partly asleep. You can explain <u>briefly</u> that he had a bad dream, and that dreams are only make-believe in his sleep, not for real.

Once he is calm, take him back to his bed; tuck him in, and stroke his back or his head as you sit next to him. Talk to him softly: tell him he will be fine, that he will be able to go to sleep safely, and that you will stay in his room until he is sound asleep. Tell him if he wakes up again, Mommy and Daddy are close by for him to call for them. Then follow the normal procedure of sitting near the child and staying in his room until he is soundly asleep.

You might also consider monitoring what your child watches on TV. This could be contributing to nightmares.

If parents will deal with nightmares in this way, the child will develop a sense of inner security; he will be able to settle down more easily each time he wakes, and eventually be able to shake off the occasional nightmares on his own, without letting them overtake him.

7.

Resist Temptation to Put Your Child in Bed With You.

Again, I want to stress for parents the importance of this. To get up and deal with your child may seem like a lot of effort for parents in the middle of the night. However, to teach the child to deal with the nighttime fears is usually simple and quickly resolved, **within two or three nights.** In the long run, it is much easier to do this for a few nights than to deal with the child getting up every night for years to come because of bad dreams.

8.

Be Aware That There Are Some Exceptions.

It should be noted that a very small percentage of children have night fears or nightmares due to previous experiences of trauma; these children may need professional help to overcome their fears. A few parents may find that their child does not respond after they have carefully attempted to train him with the procedures in this book. For such children, it may be important to get the help of a trained psychologist, and to do so as soon as possible.

For almost all little children, however, I have found that the above procedures work wonderfully, when parents realize that they can help control their child's nighttime fears and help him learn to overcome them successfully. Parents are delighted to find that they do not have to sympathize and relate to a child out of his fears, but that they can walk him out of those fears within a few short nights of effort, and create lasting results.

———◦►◄◦———

Avoiding Bedtime Tantrums 6

*I*t is typical of two-year-olds to go through a stage of saying, "No!" to everything. Some toddlers will also throw temper tantrums, particularly at bedtime. They may insist on staying up, interrupting adult evening time and refusing to go to bed.

Parents tend to waiver and falter when their child throws a big enough tantrum. They wonder if they are requiring too much of the child. When the child senses this, he quickly learns that he can manipulate his parents into letting him do what he wants, just by mustering up enough negative behavior! Such behavior is characterized by throwing himself on the floor, refusing to do what he is asked, yelling "no!" etc.

In this way, the child makes the parents feel guilty, as if Mommy and Daddy are mean, dictatorial, or demanding, simply because they have given their child a simple command to do something. However, parents need to know that it *is* OK to require compliance from a young child, and that allowing him to throw a temper tantrum is *not* OK.

Not only does your child *not* need to throw a tantrum, but he needs to know that you will remain consistent in what you require and not give in. When he realizes this, tantrums will cease; he will sense, "This will not do me any good, so why try?"

When you are about to ask your toddler to do something and you think that a temper tantrum might possibly be the result, take time to tell the child gently beforehand how he is going to think and act in the upcoming situation. Talk him through the actions you want from him before you make your request or give him direction. Before bedtime, tell your toddler how he's going to behave:

- *You are not going to fuss, even a little bit.*

- *You are going to be so happy to go to bed!*

It is important to have a plan of action before a tantrum begins. When it is time for bed, and your toddler acts as if he will begin a tantrum:

- Immediately distract the child; take him to another room, put him in a different environment, go visit the dog, take him outdoors, talk to big brother, turn on the TV, etc.

- Stay calm. Pre-determine that you will not react to him.

- Speak quietly and firmly.

- Remind him that he is not going to fuss.

- Do not waver in requiring the behavior you are trying to create.

Maintain a matter-of-fact attitude, being kind rather than reactive. There is no need to react. Be objective in your approach toward the child, and take the attitude, "Nevertheless, this is the way it is going to be."

When you don't waver, your child will sense that you mean what you say, and he will know that a tantrum will not work. Training a "difficult" child will require more planning and more fortitude on the part of the parent in order to establish in the child's thinking that "this is the way it is going to be." A thorough preparation in both the child *and* the parents is required to confidently establish the desired behavior.

Put him in bed, and then *thank* him for each little step he accomplishes. This gives him a sense of finality in the form of a pleasant and unexpected surprise. He will think, "Oh! Okay." It also gives him a sense that you trust him to do what you ask. For example, if he looks like he will get up, say calmly, "Put your little head down. Thank you." This will show him that you know he will comply, and most often he will do so.

It is important to note that if the procedures in the previous chapters are followed, most bedtime tantrums will be eliminated.

Staying Dry All Night

*I*t can be difficult for the parent to help a child change a negative behavior involving a physical function such as bedwetting, because in reality it is the child who is in control of his own body functions, rather than the parent.

However, with a great deal of nurturing, careful guidance, and using the simple approach outlined below, parents can expect dry nights, and children can experience the self-reward of success. This method has worked for hundreds of parents dealing with bedwetting, and it can work for you, too.

Often parents question whether or not their child is *physically* able to stay dry throughout the night. If this is a question in your mind, an examination by a pediatrician can determine the answer. Once it is certain that there are no physical problems causing the bedwetting (such as food allergies, kidney problems, etc.), then you can begin the procedure below. It is helpful for parents to know that most children by age two are fully capable of holding their bladders for several hours at night. You will, of course, want to follow the information in the previous chapters about bedtime routine, and limit liquids before bed, etc.

1.
Study Your Child's Wetting Pattern.

Does your child wet early in the night or just before he wakes in the morning? Is he a heavy sleeper who simply cannot awaken enough to go to the bathroom on his own? Is he unaware that he has wet until he wakes the next morning? To determine his pattern, you may need to take a couple of nights and wake yourself up every couple of hours to check him. Once you have determined his pattern, follow the procedures below, beginning with the first night of his training.

2.
Praise Your Child.
It is important to create in your child a real desire to cooperate in his training *before the training begins.* Before the first "training" night, and throughout your bedtime routine, talk to him about your expectations. The best way to do this is by using praise. *Remember, it is your most powerful tool.*

3.
Wake Your Child.
Once you have established a pattern of what time of night he is most likely to wet the bed, you will need to get up about that time of night to *wake the child before he wets* and take him to the bathroom. The purpose for this is that you are **helping him to succeed**, by blocking the "negative" behavior pattern *before* it happens; you are supporting him and helping him be successful in the new behavior of staying dry.

Not only can little children hold their bladders at night; they can also pee "on command" when they are taken to the potty. You may need to pick up your child while he is still asleep, and take him to the bathroom; let him sit on the toilet a minute or two, even though he may hardly be awake. If he does not wet, do not make a big deal of it; keep it positive, and simply put him back to bed, letting him know he can try again later. Repeat this procedure as often as needed throughout the night until he successfully urinates in the potty; then put him back to bed.

4.
Plan a
Reward.

Use a reward as a means of obtaining cooperation from the child. Again, as previously discussed, you will need to buy and wrap a small toy or favorite item, and have it ready ahead of time. Then the first night you can tell the child, "If you wake up dry in the morning, you will get a little present."

However, if he wakes wet, of course you do not give the reward. Neither should you act discouraged, and certainly do not punish him. Do not sympathize with the child and tell him, "That's all right!" This confuses him, because he knows it is not OK. Rather, take the attitude that together you will work at it until you have succeeded. Your attitude should be, "Maybe tomorrow. We can give it another try the next day!" Then let it go, drop the conversation, and do not focus on his bed-wetting. Involve him with cleaning up the sheets and clothing; even a two-year-old should help take things to the laundry room.

5.
*Succeed
Serveral
Times.*
Once he has been successful in waking dry, the stage is set for the next night. He will become more and more adept at staying dry during the night. He will have had the experience of being dry and the experience of your excitement and trust in him. Each success builds upon the next, and within three nights, he will most likely have established the pattern of "dryness."

6.
Celebrate.
After his first successful night, give him loads of verbal praise the next morning. Have an on-going celebration throughout the next couple of days until the pattern is set. As previously mentioned, give the little gift only once or twice. You don't want to create a dependency upon the reward; rather, you want the child to have the personal reward of feeling good about himself. Usually after three or four days, the child has received enough positive reinforcement to maintain the pattern. This is a good time to start backing off a little at a time, leaving the initiative more and more up to him. He has experienced the success of staying dry all night. This is usually enough to propel him into staying dry from now on!

7.
*Maintain
the New
Behavior.*
Once he is successful in staying dry throughout the night, be vigilant to help him maintain that success. If he should have an accident, do not punish him or make a big deal of it; this could be an isolated incident. If it continues for several consecutive nights, back up and go through this procedure again, step by step, until you get him back on track. Let him

know he can do it, and that you trust him and believe in him. You will see success when you create an atmosphere for the child's self-esteem and self-worth.

Questions and Answers 8

While training your toddler for bedtime, there may be additional questions or issues that arise for parents. Here are some commonly asked questions and time-proven solutions that will help you.

1. Question: How long will the training process take for new bedtime behaviors?

The normal training period using this method is only two to three days of concentrated focus on the part of parents.

Realize that from that point on, you will need only to maintain the behavior by monitoring your child, normally for about three weeks. This time period requires progressively less and less of your time.

If a child regresses after a few weeks to his previous behavior, simply begin again to monitor him and follow the procedures in these chapters.

Remember to avoid training the child in a new behavior when there is stress in the family. For example, avoid times when your toddler is sick, when he is missing Daddy who is out of town, or when the family has recently moved to a new home.

2. *Question: When should we allow our toddler to sleep with us?*

Parents enjoy snuggling in Mom and Dad's bed with their children as a time of special warmth. These times are important for the family and are needed by your children. However, our experience has shown that these times should always be based on the parents' initiative, rather than the child's demands.

Many parents allow their child to get in bed with them, without having any particular rules or a plan for the family bed. They do not realize that, without guidelines for their toddler, they are setting a pattern which allows the child to become demanding of the space and time of others.

Setting guidelines will help meet the needs of your child. Early childhood is the optimal time for setting patterns for your child's life, including how to relate to others with trust and respect. By teaching your child to sleep in his own bed, you are helping him learn to have his own center, to value his own space, and to respect your space. Children are more secure in a parent-centered family than they are in a child-centered family. For your child's development, it is important for him to know that Mom and Dad have a life of their own, together.

Setting guidelines will also help meet the needs of the parents. After a child is born, it is important that the parents continue to view each other as one another's primary relationship. To guard your relationship and keep your marriage from deteriorating, parents need to set aside certain times for snuggling with children, and certain times for adult snuggling. This is important for both you and your child.

In a healthy marriage, parents take time for each other and guard their times of intimacy. If a child is allowed to demand attention at bedtime, it can place stress on a marriage and the parents may no longer feel exclusive in their own relationship.

A child who violates Mom and Dad's space and time is no fun to live with, and allowing him to do so will lead to resentment in the parents. One of the best things parents can give their children is an awareness of the love they have for each other as husband and wife.

When to invite your child into your bed – You may wish to put your toddler in bed with you for a short time as a part of his bedtime routine. You may also want to do so at other more spontaneous times, such as in the morning when your toddler wakes up. This might be a type of reward for the child when he has slept in his own bed all night. However, once again, these times should be only at your invitation. You as the parent need to be the one who initiates it. Do not do so if the child asks, but rather tell him, "Only when Daddy and Mommy say." This way, the parent remains in control. This will set a pattern in his little mind that, "Mommy and Daddy let me get in their bed at certain special times, *not* because of *my* demands."

However, be sure you do establish a regular routine of including your toddler in a special family snuggle time, preferably a regular time each day.

3. *Question: What can I do for a child who is difficult to train?*

Only a small percentage of children experience difficulty with the training methods included in this book. If your child is experiencing difficulty and is not trained in these bedtime procedures within three days or so, it is recommended that you:

1. Examine your own attitudes toward the child. You need a positive attitude in order to help your child change.

2. Re-read and follow these procedures carefully.

3. After several attempts at training a difficult child, one strategy might be is to express *some* disappointment. You will need to be careful about what you are creating in the child if you use a negative strategy such as this. In most cases, the praise and reward that you give your child is enough.

4. If you still have difficulty, you might consider the possibility of ADD/ADHD or some other type of learning disability. If you suspect this, consult a professional. These types of children can and do learn bedtime procedures, but it takes a great deal more time and effort on the part of the parents. Realize that it will simply take more diligence, but do not give up. You do not want to give your child the underlying message, "You can't do it." Rather, you want to instill in this child early in life that there is never a problem that cannot be transcended.

For any difficult child, you will need to be diligent. Be creative. Think of new strategies until something clicks for your toddler, and you are able to keep this child moving toward the goal. Keep in mind that three is the magic number. Most often, in three days a child will have mastered a new behavior. With the more challenging child, it may take three weeks. Often the time that you are ready to quit is the time when the breakthrough is just around the corner. For the sake of the child's own feelings of self-worth, do not give up. Remain persistent, without pressuring the child; help him feel that he can be successful. He should feel that you are with him and that you trust him to be able to make this new step. Above all, he should always feel that you love him.

4. **Question: What if my child continues to wet the bed during the night?**

With the procedures discussed, most children will learn to stay dry at night in a short time. However, there is always a small percentage of children who take a little longer to attain their self-control. When bed-wetting goes on too long, it becomes a negative experience and a sense of defeat for the child. You can prevent this experience of defeat by talking with your child and telling him, "There is always a way. I know you can do this." Never let him think that you don't believe in him.

Persist in using the procedures described here consistently for a minimum of three weeks. If after three weeks the child has not responded and the training time is becoming a negative experience, consider the following approach, *only* as a temporary solution for a week or two: allow the child to use the pull-up type diapers, while meanwhile you are continuing to implement the procedures for training him to stay dry. It is very important to continue and not abandon the training. This provides two benefits: (1) Pull-up diapers can give the struggling child a feeling of accomplishment. (2) Continuing (not abandoning) the training tells the child that you really do believe he can stay dry all night.

Conclusion

O nce your child has mastered any of these new bedtime behaviors, he will gain a sense of success. Whether it is following a nighttime routine; learning to sleep in his new bed instead of a crib; overcoming nighttime fears or tantrums; or staying dry all night, mastering any of these behaviors will yield definite benefits for both you and your toddler. Parents will quickly discover that the results are well worth the temporary effort required for a few short days and nights.

However wonderful the immediate rewards of training your toddler might be, the long-term rewards are even greater. Parents will come to realize that the successes gained during the toddler years lay a foundation for building *lifetime* patterns of success.

As you follow the principles in this book, you are setting requirements; you are teaching your toddler to take responsibility for his actions; and you are helping him to experience a sense of mastery. All of this will go far toward teaching values and creating a well-adjusted, functional adult.

A toddler who masters simple procedures for bedtime will become a delight in your home, not only during his early years, but throughout his childhood and teen years.

May you discover the rewards that many parents have experienced with these methods. May these principles guide you on your parenting journey, and empower you with the realization that parents have the ability – and the responsibility – to mold and create a wonderful little human being!